CROSS TRAINING

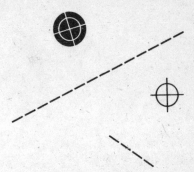

CROSS TRAINING

RANDY SOUTHERN

VICTOR BOOKS®

A DIVISION OF SCRIPTURE PRESS PUBLICATIONS INC.
USA CANADA ENGLAND

Other Young Teen Feedback Electives

CHARACTER WITNESSES
FAMILY SURVIVAL GUIDE
FOR REAL PEOPLE ONLY
FRIENDS: WHO NEEDS THEM?
HIGHER LOVE
IT CAME FROM THE MEDIA
NOBODY LIKE ME
THE SCHOOL ZONE
WHAT'S YOUR PROBLEM?
WHEN EVERYONE'S LOOKING AT YOU

Leader's books available for group study.

Scripture quotations are from the *Holy Bible, New International Version*, © 1973, 1978, 1984, International Bible Society. Used by permission of Zondervan Bible Publishers.

Library of Congress Catalog Card Number:
90-70898
ISBN: 0-89693-285-0

  2 3 4 5 6 7 8 9 10 Printing/Year 94 93 92

CONTENTS

GUTS AND GLORY

CHAPTER ONE

This is a book about living the Christian life: what it means and why it's important. But before we get into that, we need to get some things straight. There are a lot of myths currently being passed off as truth by well-meaning Christians. I'd like to begin by addressing six of the most dangerous ones.

MYTH #1: GOD IS INTERESTED IN OUR PERSONAL LIVES

This belief is the result of man's enormous ego. Man believes that everything should center on him. God — the most important and powerful Being in the universe — is *not* interested in every little thing that goes on in every person's life. He's got much more important, universal matters to attend to.

God created the original "ball of matter" and then let it evolve into the universe as we know it. In the same process, man evolved. God wasn't directly involved in the process, but He was the Originator. Today God maintains a "hands-off" approach — He is aware of what goes on, but He isn't actively involved.

Whatever happens in this life is up to us. It's foolish to blame God for the things that go wrong and ask Him to make them right. It's also foolish to think that everything that goes right is due to "God's blessing." People who think that way are living out a fantasy.

MYTH #2: JESUS IS THE SON OF GOD

This myth was created by some early Bible scholars who took some of Jesus' quotes out of context. If you examine the Bible closely, you'll find that Jesus never once claimed to be the Son of God. The reason is simple: He wasn't.

What He was was the greatest teacher the world has ever seen. His ideas were so radical and so brilliant that they are still being taught around the world today. His speaking style was so moving and so persuasive that enormous crowds followed Him wherever He went.

It's only natural that as Jesus' fame and popularity spread, people began to circulate rumors and exaggerations about Him and the things He did. Some of the rumors were based on misunderstandings, such as the one concerning the wedding feast at which He supposedly turned water into wine. Others, however, were just outrageous nonsense, such as the claims that He healed blind people and brought the dead back to life.

Christians who still believe such rumors today are trying to bring the supernatural into what is otherwise a practical religion.

MYTH #3: JESUS ROSE FROM THE DEAD

There is no doubt that Jesus was put to death on a cross. The historical records are quite clear about that.

Roman officials and Jewish leaders grew tired of hearing Him incite crowds to rebel against their authority and tradition. So, after He ignored several of their warnings to stop, they had Him captured, tried Him, and crucified Him.

And that's the end of the story.

Unfortunately, there were followers back then who couldn't bear the thought of Christ's being dead, so they staged an elaborate hoax to make it seem as if He had come back to life.

A few days after His death, they stole His body from its grave. Then, for the next month or so, they reported seeing Him in different places. When several such reports were made, Roman officials decided to investigate.

Conveniently, when they started their investigation, the followers suddenly announced that Jesus was gone—that He had ascended into heaven.

This myth has been handed down from generation to generation, and is still widely believed today, despite several scholarly findings which have disproved it.

Again, people who hold on to this myth are trying to find some magical answer to help them escape from life's everyday problems.

MYTH #4: THE BIBLE IS GOD'S WORD

The Bible is a great book. It's a tremendous resource for studying ancient cultures. The view of history it presents is unlike any other. Its stories and legends of ancient heroes and villains make for interesting reading even today. And it offers some good principles on how to live.

But it's not God's Word. It wasn't inspired by God. It was created in the minds of men. People who believe that it came directly from God are deceiving themselves. They would be just as well off to put their faith in Mother Goose.

MYTH #5: SATAN EXISTS

Santa Claus, the Tooth Fairy, and the devil—what do they have in common? They don't exist.

In prehistoric times, man made up the idea of an evil being to explain the bad things that happened to him. This idea was passed down through the ages and is still very popular today.

Blaming all our problems on some fantasy figure with a pointed tail and horns is as ridiculous as it sounds. Christians who believe that Satan exists are merely trying to pass the blame for their own sins.

MYTH #6: NON-CHRISTIANS GO TO HELL

There are a lot of Christians who believe that, unless a person accepts

Christ as "personal Saviour," he or she will go to hell forever. Yet most of these same Christians would say that God is love.

They don't seem to recognize that *both* of these statements can't be true. If God is love, He wouldn't send someone to hell. *If* there is an afterlife, *everyone* will spend it in heaven.

The idea of hell was created by some narrow-minded early Christians to scare people into believing as they did. It is an idea that should not be continued today.

THE EXPLANATION
When you look at Christianity from a logical, scientific point of view, it makes much more sense, doesn't it?

I hope you said no. Because everything I've written in this book so far is a lie! I hope that as soon as you read each myth, you rejected it because you knew better.

The *real* truth is that: God *is* interested

in our personal lives; Jesus *did* claim to be and *is* the Son of God; Christ *did* rise from the dead; the Bible *is* God's Word; Satan *does* exist; and people who reject Christ *will* go to hell.

This first chapter probably isn't what you expected, is it? I wanted to surprise you because I wanted to get a point across. The point is that there are people in this world — so-called "experts" — who believe that Christianity is nothing more than a bunch of myths.

And these experts can be convincing.

That's why it's important for us Christians to be deeply rooted in our beliefs. We need to know what we believe and why we believe it.

And beyond that, we need to make our beliefs personal. We must know in our minds and hearts, through our own personal relationship with Christ and our own knowledge of God's Word, that what we believe is the truth. In other words, we need an unshakable, personal faith.

The rest of this book is designed to

help you establish a personal faith.

Please read on.

HOW TO READ THE BIBLE — WITHOUT FALLING ASLEEP

CHAPTER TWO

When was the last time you sat down, popped open your Bible, immediately became interested in what you were reading, and studied intently for the next two hours?

(For me, I think it was about the same time that I got heat stroke at the North Pole.)

The simple fact is — studying the Bible can be hard work.

It's not always easy to read God's Word, is it? Some people want us to believe that all we have to do is open the Bible, close our eyes, and point to a verse, and God will suddenly reveal a magnificent truth to us.

That doesn't happen very often. Instead, we usually have to dig hard for His truth. It's not easy—but it's certainly worth it. When you begin to discover some of the amazing things in the Bible, you'll see how "worth it" it is.

But how do I dig for these truths, you may be asking. *How do I study the Bible?*

Good questions. As a matter of fact, those were the exact same questions facing Mrs. Sorensen's Sunday School class. Mrs. S. had been teaching for several weeks on the importance of having a regular personal Bible study time. Five of her students decided to give it a try. Let's look at how each one of her students went about his or her study and see if we can pick up some do's and don'ts.

McLAIN'S METHOD

McLain's Bible study method was to read when he "felt led to." If he sat down to read and somehow got sidetracked, he decided that it wasn't the right time to read. He felt that it was dishonoring to God to let his mind wander while he was studying. So whenever something interrupted his concentration while he read, he would stop reading and come back to it another time when his mind was clearer. But because there are so many things going on in McLain's life, he hasn't been able to complete a study time in almost three months.

McLain's desire to focus *all* of his attention on the Bible when he studies is great. The problem is the way he goes about it. Concentrating when we study isn't easy. Satan doesn't want us in God's Word, so he'll throw all kinds of distractions at us. And if he can get us to put our Bibles down in frustration, he's won the battle.

The way to fight Satan is to go over his head—with prayer. As you study, ask God to keep your mind focused. He'll help you. He wants you to study His Word.

But be warned: Satan doesn't give up easily. He'll keep throwing distractions at you. You may find that you need to pray two or three times during your study. That's fine—however many times it takes to keep your mind focused on God's Word.

LINDSAY'S METHOD

Lindsay was excited about her Bible study method. Mrs. S. had given her a bookmark that showed how you could read through the whole Bible in one year. So, each morning when she got up, Lindsay would read a certain number of chapters and verses from the Old Testament. And, before she went to bed at night, she would read a certain number of chapters and verses from the New Testament.

After she read a chapter, she would check it off in her Bible. She felt a sense of accomplishment every time she checked off a chapter. Once in a while she would flip back through her Bible to see just how much she'd read.

But the problem was, on Sundays, when Mrs. S. would ask what everyone got out of his or her Bible study, Lindsay didn't know how to answer. She didn't really *get anything* out of her study. She just read. Most days she couldn't even remember what she'd read the day before.

Why isn't Lindsay getting anything from her study?

It's because of the way she approaches Bible study. Her goal is to get through a certain number of verses every day. The problem with that goal is that it causes her to focus on what she's getting done rather than on what she's reading.

Rather than trying to discover what she can learn about God in the passage she's reading, Lindsay often looks ahead to see how many more verses she has to read. Getting through the passage is more important to her than learning something from it.

You've heard the old saying: "It's not the quantity, it's the quality." This can apply to Lindsay. It's great that she's committed to daily Bible study—but God doesn't care whether we read through the Bible in one year or not. He wants us to discover (and savor) the truths He's put in the Bible—even if it takes us 27 years!

KEN'S METHOD

Ken's study method was a little like Lindsay's. He decided he would read a chapter of the Bible a day. Unlike Lindsay, he really tried to concentrate on what he was reading and discover all the truths that he could find. But some of those chapters have a lot of stuff in them! (He almost fainted one night when he opened to Psalm 119 and saw that it had 176 verses.) He couldn't concentrate on every truth he discovered in a chapter because there were so many. So he usually ended the study frustrated and irritated.

Maybe Lindsay and Ken should get together and talk about that "quality and quantity" stuff.

Trying to get through a whole chapter in each study is way too much. No wonder Ken was frustrated.

A better approach is to pick out one or two verses—a paragraph at the most—

and study them. Read the passage. Re-read it. Then read it again. Think about it. What advice in the verse could apply to your life? What lessons can you learn from the characters in the passage? How does it relate to another verse you've already read?

God created our minds — He knows how they work. For that reason, He put a lot of His wisdom into "bite-sized chunks" so it would be easier to understand.

CHARLI'S METHOD

Charli started her study in a logical way. *The Bible is a book,* she reasoned. *You read a book by starting at the beginning and reading page by page to the end.* So that's how Charli studied.

At first, it wasn't too bad. Genesis was interesting, with the Creation and the Flood and all that. And Exodus was OK, although it kind of dragged at the end. She barely made it through Leviticus.

And then came . . . Numbers.

By the time she got to "These were the names of the Gershonite clans: Libni and Shimei. The Kohathite clans: Amram, Ishar, Hebron and Uzziel . . ." her eyes were glazed over.

Charli's right—the Bible is a book. But it doesn't have to be read straight through to be understood. In fact, trying to read it straight through may be more frustrating than inspiring.

Books like Leviticus and Numbers are important (and they do make sense, believe it or not)—but they're not the best place to start a Bible study.

It's better to start out with the exciting, "interesting" books like Mark, James, and Proverbs—books that offer action and advice you can easily apply to your life today. Then, as you get more familiar with the Bible, you can move on to some of the "harder" books—and they will make sense to you!

PAUL'S METHOD

Paul had trouble beginning his Bible study. It seemed like every time he'd start studying, he'd think of something else he could be doing. But he stayed with it. When his mind started to wander, he'd stop and ask God to show him something new in the passage he was reading to help him get back on track.

He reads about a paragraph or so each night, right after he does his homework. He started out in the Book of Mark. The more he read about Jesus' life and the things He taught, the more he realized what it really means to be a Christian.

From there, Paul moved on to the Book of James, where he picked up some valuable tips on how to control his tongue (something he's had problems with lately).

Now he's just started in the Book of Proverbs, and he's amazed at how a book written over 3,000 years ago can have so much information and instruction that still applies today.

Don't get the wrong idea about Paul. He's not some spiritual giant or some Bible bookworm. He's a regular person, just like you. And he's discovering that the Bible can make a lot of sense and be very helpful to regular people.

No one can determine what the best Bible study method for you is except you. You've just seen five different examples of Bible study. Perhaps you've seen some things in these examples that you'd like to build into your Bible study. And perhaps you've seen some other things that you'd like to avoid. That's great.

The important thing isn't *how* you study; the important thing is *that* you study.

GOING THE DISTANCE
CHAPTER THREE

Do you ever wish that you'd lived during the time of Christ? Don't you think it would have been a lot easier to be a Christian back then? You could have followed Jesus around in person and heard Him preach and teach. You could have actually seen Him heal blind people and raise the dead. If you didn't understand something that He said, you could have asked Him about it on the spot. And, perhaps best of all, you could have been an eyewitness to His Resurrection!

Yeah, when you think about it, it would have been great to have lived back then.

Or, better yet—what if Christ were alive today? What if He lived, preached, and taught in your hometown? What if you could go to Him anytime in person to ask Him a question or to get His advice about a problem? Think about it—wouldn't it be great if we had direct access to Christ today?

We do. We have the Bible.

Let me explain.

ONE LAST PROMISE

Just before Jesus ascended into heaven to complete His work on earth, He made a final promise to His followers:

"I am with you always, to the very end of the age" (Matthew 28:20).

Since Jesus was on His way to heaven as He spoke those words, He obviously wasn't talking about being with us *physically*. So what did He mean?

How could He say He's with us if He's in heaven?

27

Actually, He's with us in three different forms.

First, He's with us in the form of the Holy Spirit. The Holy Spirit dwells in the heart of every believer. As Christians, we are to be "filled with the Spirit" (Ephesians 5:18). That means allowing the Spirit to occupy, guide, and control every area of our lives. This fullness is one way Christ is with us.

Second, He's with us in the form of prayer. We have instant access to Him anytime. His line's never busy, He's always home, He's always happy to hear from us, and He's always willing to listen and talk.

And third, He's with us in the form of the Bible. Throughout Scripture, Jesus is identified very closely with the Bible. John went so far as to call Jesus "the Word" (John 1:1).

Jesus *is* with us today in the form of the Bible. That means that most of the questions and problems we would like to take to Him in person can be answered in the Bible—if we only take the time to look.

GOD'S WORD — THINK ABOUT IT

"The Bible is God's Word." How many times have you heard that? The phrase is used so often that it can become like "The Star-Spangled Banner" or the Pledge of Allegiance: we know all the words, but we don't think about what they mean. Let's *do* think about what "The Bible is God's Word" means.

If my friend Randy is talking to me, what I hear are Randy's words. In the same way, when I read the Bible, what I read are God's Words. Not the words of a bunch of guys writing what they think *about* God, but God's Words.

And because it's God's Word, you know that everything in it is true. You can also be sure that any answers or advice that you get from the Bible are absolutely the best answers and advice available.

AND IT'S COMPLETE TOO

Not only is the Bible God's Word, it's His complete Word. This means that *everything* we need to know about the Christian life is found in the Bible.

We hear stories about people who practice Eastern religions traveling halfway around the world to discover some obscure truth about the meaning of life from a bald, 800-year-old monk in a cave on top of a mountain in Tibet.

Luckily, God has made it a lot easier for us. Everything that we absolutely need to know about living a life pleasing to Him, He's supplied between the covers of one Book.

That's not to say that every other Christian book ever written is worthless. Other books are helpful in explaining certain parts of the Bible and putting the Bible into context in our lives today. But these books are only Bible "helpers." They don't *add* any new truths.

STICKING WITH IT

You already know that the Bible is God's Word, of course; and if you read chapter 2 maybe you've even given some thought to how to get the most out of reading God's Word. Chances are, if you weren't serious about getting to know God better, you wouldn't be reading this chapter now.

So what's the point? The point is that the Bible is worth more than an occasional glance from time to time. It's worth a chunk of your time *regularly* — every day, ideally.

In the Bible, we have access to Jesus, and we have access to God's complete Word. And that access is as close as your bookshelf.

What are you going to do with it?

BEYOND "NOW I LAY ME DOWN TO SLEEP"

CHAPTER FOUR

June was sitting in the cafeteria. She'd brought her lunch, but for some strange reason, the "mystery meat" burgers on the school menu sounded good to her. So she bought a burger and gave the lunch her mom had packed to Kris, the new girl in school, who was sitting across the table from her.

"June, I'd like to thank you for this lunch," Kris said in a monotone voice.

"Oh, that's OK," June replied. "My mom packed—"

"And thank-you for the peanut butter

sandwich," Kris continued.

"Do you like pea—" June started.

"And thank-you for the potato chips," Kris said.

"They're really—"

"And thank-you for the Ho-Hos. And thank-you for the apple. And thank-you for the skim milk."

June watched Kris as she talked, and noticed that she really wasn't even talking to June. She was kind of muttering to herself as she peered into the lunch bag and looked around the room absentmindedly.

"Would you help me in study hall today?" Kris asked, still not looking at June. "I need help studying for the algebra quiz on Thursday."

"Sure. I'd be—" June started.

"And could you help me tomorrow after school in English so I can get a good grade?"

"Well, I guess I—"

"See ya later. Bye," Kris said as she quickly got up and walked away (still not looking at June). On her way out she threw away most of the food June had given her.

June shrugged her shoulders and watched her go.

A few hours later as June stood at her locker between classes, Kris rushed up behind her.

"I accidently broke Karen's Walkman and she wants me to pay her back for it right now," she explained urgently, glancing around as she spoke. "I need money. Will you give it to me?"

June had made some extra money baby-sitting over the weekend and didn't have any plans to spend it, so she gave Kris $35.

"Thank-you for giving me the money," Kris said as she grabbed it and hurried away. "See ya. Bye."

Later that night, as June was doing her homework, Kris called.

"June, thank-you for being my friend,"

Kris said.

"Hey, that's O—" June began.

"And thank-you for giving me your lunch."

"No prob—"

"And thank-you for giving me money. And thank-you for helping me study. And thank-you for everything you did for me today. Would you please help me with my homework tomorrow?"

"Yeah, I could—" June started.

"And would you please introduce me to your friends so I'll know people at school? And would you please walk home with me after school? . . ."

June listened to Kris talk for a while. Then, after about five minutes, there was silence.

"I'd be glad to help you, Kris," June said. "I know what it's like to be the new kid at school. If there's anything I can—"

From the other end of the line came

the unmistakable sound of snoring.

Pretty weird, huh?

How in the world can Kris expect to have any kind of friendship with June if she keeps acting this way? Kris could use a crash course in communication skills.

June would really like to be Kris' friend, but she's not sure how long she can put up with being treated this way. The only time Kris talks to her is to ask her for something or to thank her for something. And even then she doesn't act like she means it. She acts like she just says it to be polite.

And whenever June tries to talk, Kris either cuts her off, walks away . . . or falls asleep. Some relationship.

Of course this is just a fictional story. There aren't really any relationships like this. . . . Right?

"Lord, thank-You for this day and thank-You for this food and bless it to our bodies. In Jesus' name, amen."

"Lord, I forgot about this quiz. Please

help me know the answers. Amen."

"Lord, thank-You for this day and thank-You for everything You've done for me and (yawn) bless Dad tomorrow . . . as he leaves on his (yawn, blink-blink) business trip and . . . ZZZZZZ."

Any of these prayers sound familiar to you? They do to me. I've prayed hundreds of prayers just like them. How about you?

As Christians, we talk about having a "relationship" with God. The key to any relationship is communication. What kind of relationship can we have with God if we communicate with Him in half-hearted, half-asleep, ritual prayers? How would you feel if someone talked to you that way? (Remember Kris and June.)

GOD—A PERSONAL FRIEND OF MINE
What do you think of when you think of God?
(a) The Almighty Creator of the

universe.

(b) The mysterious Spirit that traveled in a cloud by day and a pillar of fire by night and spoke to the Israelites in a voice of thunder.

(c) My closest Friend.

(d) All of the above.

If you answered (d), you either have a real understanding of who God is or you figured out that (d) was the obvious answer that I was looking for.

Do you consider God to be a close friend of yours? if not, He can be. (And any friend who can part the Red Sea is a pretty good friend to have.) The key is communication.

ONE TO ONE

Here's something we don't consider very often: *Anytime* we pray, we have the most powerful Being in the world listening to our every word. He *loves* it when we talk to Him! And not only that, He loves to talk to us! He wants to have a relationship with us.

Is that an incredible opportunity or

what? So why is it that so many of us blow it with prayers like, "Now I lay me down to sleep . . ."?

It's because we don't understand what prayer is.

Prayer isn't some short speech we make before meals and bedtime. Prayer is conversation with a Friend.

PRAYER TIPS

No one can tell you exactly how you should communicate with God. Your relationship with Him is between the two of you. But there are some principles which can make your time with Him more profitable. Here are a few of them for you to think about.

- *Praise Him.* You know how good it feels when one of your friends says something nice about you. Compliments and praise are great ways to build friendships. Thank God for something He's done or praise Him for something you noticed about His character that day. You'll have a lot of things to choose from. Pick one or two that stand out in your mind.

- *Bring any relationship barriers out into the open.* If one of your friends does something to hurt you, you'll probably have a hard time talking to that person until he or she apologizes to you and asks your forgiveness. The same is true with God. Because He's perfect and because He wants His best for us, when we sin, we hurt Him deeply. And we make it hard to talk to Him. To remove the barrier, we need to apologize for what we did and ask His forgiveness.

- *When you ask Him for something, recognize whom you are talking to.* God is a unique Friend. When you talk to Him, you are talking to Someone who knows exactly what you need to be perfectly happy forever. He knows much more about what will make you happy than you do. Remember that. When you ask Him for something, don't ask for what you *think* you need, ask Him for what He *knows* you need.

- *Listen.* Don't hog all the conversation. Let God talk. He *will* talk to you. He does it in several ways: through His Word—the Bible; through His Holy Spirit's "still, small voice" in your heart—your conscience; through allowing or not allowing certain circumstances to occur, etc. If you're truly listening for it, you'll hear God's voice talking to you.

- *Pray anytime.* Don't think you can pray only when you're locked in your room, alone, in your set-aside prayer time (although it is important to have a daily, set-aside prayer time). God is your Friend. Talk to Him anytime. If you see a sunset that you like a lot, thank Him for it. If you have a fight with one of your other friends, ask His advice about what to do. If you're unsure about some decision you have to make, tell Him about it. He's always there.

Oh, and before you leave this chapter—there's Someone here who'd like to talk to you.

CHRIST STILL HAS A BODY

CHAPTER FIVE

Let me ask you a personal question.

Have you ever had an ingrown toenail? If you have, you'll know the kind of pain I'm talking about. If you haven't, let me try to explain it.

The medical definition of an ingrown toenail is one that grows *into* the skin, rather than out of it, thus irritating the nerve endings. My personal definition of an ingrown toenail is a pain so intense it will make you wet your pants.

Unless you've experienced the pain, there's no way you can understand how much an ingrown toenail hurts. Many professional football players, who normally wouldn't miss a game for anything less than an amputation, have been sidelined by ingrown toenails.

Because of the location of the pain, any pressure on the toe, or the foot, or the leg, etc., is unbearable. Walking becomes almost impossible, and sometimes even *breathing* makes it hurt.

In summary, an ingrown toenail hurts—a lot.

THE SMALL SOURCE
OF BIG PAIN

"Well, that's great," you may be saying (with more than a little sarcasm in your voice). "Thanks for telling me about ingrown toenails. That was really interesting. Maybe next chapter you can talk about gall bladder surgery."

The point I'm trying to make is that tremendous pain can come from a tiny source. If you were to rank body parts in order of how important they are, toenails would probably be down at the bottom of the list along with nose hairs and earlobes. It would be safe to say that toenails are almost . . . insignificant.

And yet, when this insignificant part is not functioning properly, the effects are felt thoughout the entire body.

A BUNCH OF BODY PARTS

First Corinthians 12:12-27 tells us that if we have accepted Christ as our Saviour—if we claim to be Christians—we are in the "body of Christ."

And just as our human bodies are made up of different parts, so is the body of Christ. *We* are those parts. *We* make up Christ's body on earth.

Each and every Christian—including you and me—is a part of the body of Christ. How does that make you feel?

Many times our first reaction is to brush off the responsibility. We might say something like, "Well, if I am a part of the body, I'm a very unimportant one."

Think about the toenail. It's "unimportant" too. But think of the pain it causes the whole body when it doesn't function properly. In the same way, we "unimportant" parts can hurt the entire body of Christ if we don't perform *our* functions properly.

It sounds pretty extreme, I know. But it's true. The parts of the body depend on each other. If one part fails, it affects the other parts.

THE FUNCTIONS OF THE PARTS

Some of you now may be asking an obvious question: "How can I perform my function *if I don't know what it is?* Good question.

But before we answer it, it would be helpful to explain the purpose of the body of Christ in general. When Christ left the earth and ascended into heaven, He assigned to His followers the task of carrying on His work and spreading His message throughout the world. That today is still the job of the body of Christ. That is the goal all of its parts, working together, should be striving for.

Just as in the human body, the parts of the body of Christ each have a specific function. And obviously, we have to know what our specific function is before we can perform it.

HOW DO YOU DISCOVER YOUR FUNCTION?

There are two steps in discovering what your function in the Body of Christ is: (1) identifying your unique abilities and spiritual gifts; and (2) connecting with other parts of the body (fellowshipping with other Christians).

I don't mean to leave you hanging, but we'll be discussing both of these steps in detail in the next couple of chapters. For now it's enough that you recognize that:

- you are part of the body of Christ;
- as a part of the body of Christ, you have a specific job to do;
- if you don't perform your job, it affects the other parts of the Body.

AM I AN EYE OR AN EAR?

CHAPTER SIX

- Erik was born a natural leader. Usually if he decides to do something, others will follow. If he decides to goof off and crack jokes during Sunday School, most of the rest of the class will too. If he decides to pay attention, others pay attention too.

  Erik isn't bossy or cocky. He just has a natural quality about him that makes others want to associate with him. His quiet confidence causes other people to want to do what he does. Leadership is part of Erik's personality.

- Ann is often described by her

friends as generous and giving. If one of her friends is sick, Ann can be counted on to be there with a get-well card. On her friends' birthdays, she buys them small presents and makes them feel special. And on weekends in the mall, she can usually be counted on to treat a friend or two to frozen yogurt.

But she's not only generous with her *money*, she's also generous with her time and energy. She's never too busy to help a friend with homework or to baby-sit the neighbors' kids when they need a night out. Although a few people may try to take advantage of Ann's giving spirit, her real friends recognize and appreciate it. Generosity is part of Ann's personality.

- Ever since he got his first set of Legos, Cliff has been good with his hands. Everything he builds—from model rockets to birdhouses to the storage shed in his family's backyard—has a special quality to it.

Not only is Cliff good at working with his hands, he *enjoys* it. He has just as much fun helping his dad roof the house or rebuilding the carburetor of his car as he does playing basketball or watching a movie. Craftsmanship is part of Cliff's personality.

- Talking to Carl could make anyone feel better. He's that type of guy. Anytime one of his friends has a problem, Carl is there to listen and offer encouragement. He doesn't have all the answers, and he doesn't claim to. He just listens.

People can share things with him without worrying that he'll tell someone else about it. They also don't have to worry that he'll think less of them for what they tell him. He is always accepting and non-judgmental. He's easy to talk to. Listening and encouragment are part of Carl's personality.

You probably know people with abilities and personalities similar to Erik, Ann, Cliff, and Carl. Do you ever think of them as having "spiritual gifts"? They do.

And what about you? What abilities and personal characteristics do you have that other people notice? What are your spiritual gifts?

BREAKING THE MYTH OF SPIRITUAL GIFTS

Too often when we think of "spiritual gifts," we think of things like healing, preaching, and prophecy. And we assume that only certain people have spiritual gifts.

That's simply not the case! God has given *all Christians* spiritual gifts. Whether we choose to recognize them and put them to use is up to us.

WHAT EXACTLY ARE SPIRITUAL GIFTS?

A spiritual gift is any special ability or personal characteristic given by God to a believer that can be used in the body of Christ. As we saw in the four examples at the beginning of the chapter, they can be attributes that we may take for granted, without realizing their spiritual potential.

It would be a shame—and a waste of God's presents—for people to miss out on using their spiritual gifts because they didn't recognize what those gifts were. For that reason, let's look briefly at some of the different spiritual gifts. As you read about each different gift, ask yourself, "Could I possibly have this gift?"

- TEACHING—The ability to understand, clearly explain, and apply the Word of God to the lives of listeners.

- CREATIVE COMMUNICATION—The ability to communicate God's truth through a variety of art forms.

- ENCOURAGEMENT—The ability to reassure, strengthen, and affirm people who are discouraged or wavering in their faith.

- EVANGELISM—The ability to effectively communicate the message of Christ to unbelievers.

- HOSPITALITY—The ability to care for needy people by providing fellowship, food, or shelter.

- LEADERSHIP—The ability to attract, lead, and motivate people to accomplish the work of the ministry.

- MERCY—The ability to minister cheerfully and appropriately to people who are suffering.

- CRAFTSMANSHIP—The ability to create and construct necessary tools for ministry.

- GIVING—The ability to contribute money and material resources cheerfully to the work of the Lord.

- HELPS—The ability to perform physical tasks within the body of Christ.

YOUR SPIRITUAL GIFTS

Did any of these gifts sound familiar to you? Could you picture yourself as having any of them? Chances are, you possess at least one of the gifts on the list, if not more.

It's not difficult to discover what your spiritual gifts are. Think for a moment about the abilities and characteristics you have that you are most proud of. What are you good at? What interests you? What aspects of your character do your friends and family recognize and appreciate most? It's a good guess that your responses to these questions include some of your spiritual gifts.

God didn't bury our spiritual gifts deep down inside us so that we have to dig to find them. Instead, He's made most of them pretty obvious on the surface of our personalities.

That's not to say that you'll automatically know every spiritual gift you possess right away. Some may not become obvious for a few years. Others you may have to work hard to develop over a period of time.

But you've probably identified one or two gifts that you possess now. If so, it's time to put them to use.

GOOD INVESTMENTS

CHAPTER SEVEN

Next time you watch a professional football game, pay close attention to the individual players. I know that sounds kind of obvious, but it's not. Often when we watch a game, we focus on the end result of a play — whether or not it was a touchdown, a first down, a sack, etc.

Or if we *do* focus on an individual, it's usually because he made an outstanding play or an incredibly stupid mistake. We notice the flashy, "high-profile" parts of the game.

But if you look closely at a professional football game on any given play, you'll see 22 men, each performing a specific task to help his team. And you'll also notice that if one man doesn't perform his task, the whole play can be ruined. For instance, if the wide receiver cuts *left* instead of right, the quarterback's throw will likely be intercepted. Or, if an offensive lineman doesn't block his defensive man, the quarterback is dead meat.

Each task—no matter how small—is important to the play. And each team member is equally responsible for the success of the team.

You'll also notice that each player has certain characteristics which help him fulfill his task on the field. The center is quick and powerful, which enables him to snap the ball to the quarterback and block his defensive man all in one motion. The wide receiver is fast and has "good hands," which helps him get open and catch the passes thrown his way. The quarterback has good peripheral vision and a strong arm, which helps him spot potential receivers downfield and get the ball to them in a hurry. The different abilities and characteristics of these players work together to form a successful team.

THE BODY OF CHRIST: JUST LIKE A FOOTBALL TEAM

We've already discussed how all Christians are part of the body of Christ. Now let's carry it a bit further and see how the body of Christ is like a football team. (I know it sounds weird, but it really is a helpful way to illustrate how each of us fits into the body of Christ.)

Just like football players, Christians are part of a team. And just like the individual members of a football team, each Christian has a specific task to perform. The ultimate success of the "team" depends on each member's performing his or her task—whether it seems important at the time or not.

In the last chapter, we looked at some of the different spiritual gifts available to Christians. From that, I hope you decided on one or two gifts that you feel you have.

(If you haven't done that yet, it would be helpful for you to go back and do it now. The rest of us will wait for you. . . .)

PUTTING 'EM TO USE

So you have an idea of what your spiritual gifts are. Great. Now it's time to put them into practice.

Perhaps when you first recognized what your gifts are, you thought of a great way to put them to use in your church. If so, that's fantastic. Go to it. But if you looked at your gifts and asked yourself, "What in the world can I do with them?"—don't worry.

Here are a few steps you can take to find out how to put your spiritual gifts to use.

• The first, and most obvious thing to do is pray. Ask the Lord to open up opportunities for you to use your gifts. He created them in you and He'll certainly help you to use them.

• Second, talk to your parents or some other mature Christian whose opinion you respect. Explain what you feel your gifts are and ask their advice on how you can best use those gifts. Their advice can give you an idea of where to begin in your quest to put your gifts to use.

- Third, talk with your youth group leader. Chances are, he or she will have several ideas about how you can use your gifts in the youth group.

- And fourth, talk with your pastor. He will be able to give some ideas as to how your gifts can benefit the whole church, as well as your local community.

FOR INSTANCE

In the last chapter we looked at 10 specific spiritual gifts. Using those same 10 categories, let's now look at some specific ways each gift may be used. Of course, every church is different and these suggestions may not apply to you. That's OK. The point I'm trying to make is that every spiritual gift can be used in a practical way.

- TEACHING — You could assist a Sunday School teacher in teaching some of the younger kids in the church. By starting as an assistant, you wouldn't be faced with the pressure of preparing a lesson each week, and you would have an opportunity to learn about teaching from someone who is more experienced.

- **CREATIVE COMMUNICATION**—You could help publicize your youth group's next fund-raising event by creating an eye-catching sign or flyer. Of you could write and/or perform a skit for your youth group or as a part of your church's worship service.

- **ENCOURAGEMENT**—You could find out from your youth pastor the name of someone in your group who may be struggling for some reason, and establish regular, supportive communication with that person.

- **EVANGELISM**—You could begin a monthly outreach program in which members of your youth group travel to a local mall to share their faith with strangers they meet.

- **HOSPITALITY**—You could volunteer a few hours of your spare time each week to a local organization that is dedicated to helping the homeless.

- LEADERSHIP—You could organize and lead a Bible study for interested members of your youth group.

- MERCY—You could get involved in your church's hospital visitation program.

- CRAFTSMANSHIP—You could volunteer your time and effort in your church's next building project. Or you could help repair the homes and/or cars of some of the poor and elderly people in your community.

- GIVING—You could set aside a certain portion of your allowance or paycheck each week to give to a specific church project or fund.

- HELPS—You could help clean up the sanctuary after Sunday morning service. Or you could volunteer to mow the church's lawn.

Again, it's not important that you use my ideas. What is important is that you find *some* way to effectively use your gifts.

Remember, the whole team's counting on you.

SNEAK PREVIEW
CHAPTER EIGHT

The sun is shining, it's 80 degrees out-
side, and there's not a cloud in the sky.
Most of your friends are out playing
basketball, riding bikes, or catching
some rays at the beach. It's gotta be
the most perfect day of the year.

But unfortunately, the most perfect
day of the year fell on a Sunday. And
where are you? In church.

You're wondering why you're here.
What's the point? Nothing new ever
happens here. It's the same old thing
every week.

At the door, an usher greets you and

hands you a bulletin. As you make your way inside, a few people shake your hand, smile, and tell you they're glad to see you. Inside the sanctuary, you sit down on what has to be the most uncomfortable seating device ever invented—a pew.

After a few minutes of the organ "prelude" (that's what it's called in the bulletin), the choir comes in and sings a song that was written about a thousand years ago. Then you stand and sing with the rest of the congregation a hymn with words like "didst" and "Thou" in it.

Then you sit down and listen to the assistant pastor make announcements, stand up and sing more "didst" hymns, sit down while the offering plates are passed around, then stand up for another hymn.

And then comes the sermon.

Sometimes you try to pay attention— *you really do try.* But it's practically impossible. Most of the things the pastor talks about are boring and just don't have much to do with your life. Oh, sometimes he might tell a good joke or an interesting story, but not very often.

You've got the pastor timed — you know he'll usually preach for 25–30 minutes. So you count down the minutes on your watch and hope he doesn't go long.

When he's done, you stand and sing one more hymn (usually a real slow one), and the pastor prays and dismisses you.

Then everyone does the "church shuffle" as they file out of the pews and into the narthex. No one really goes anyplace — they just keep moving their feet up and down, waiting for the person in front of them to move. At this point, a lot of people are hugging and shaking hands with each other. Then everyone shakes the pastor's hand and leaves.

And the whole thing starts over again the next Sunday.

That's how I used to feel about church. For me, it was about as exciting and meaningful as a Solitaire tournament or a bagpipe quartet.

AN AMAZING TRUTH TO THINK ABOUT

As you can tell, I didn't have a very high opinion of church. But that's because I didn't recognize what church really is. When I was younger, I thought of church as something you went to because your parents made you. Then when I got older, I thought of going to church as something you did to show how spiritual you were.

But when I learned what going to church is really about, my focus changed. Suddenly going to church made sense. I had a purpose for going, and it became an enjoyable experience for me.

And the incredible part of it is this: Now I actually *look forward* to going to church. And, if for some reason I can't attend, I actually miss being there! It's become an important part of my life.

"So what is this amazing truth about church that changed your whole perspective, Randy?"

(I was hoping you'd ask that.)

Church worship is for *God*, not for us.

GIVING A LITTLE BACK

Think about what God does for us each week. (It's impossible for our minds to conceive *everything* He does for us, so let's just think about the basics.) He gives us life, first of all. (I guess that's probably the most obvious one.) He gives us food to eat. He provides us with a place to live. He surrounds us with people who love and care about us. And, best of all, He gave us His Son so that we can be assured of eternal happiness.

(These are just the basics. If you want to get specific about what God does for us each week, you could fill a set of encyclopedias.)

I think it's safe to say that we have a lot to be thankful for. But here's a startling and exciting thought: We can show our thankfulness to God and even give something *back* to Him — our worship.

Of course we could never begin to *re-*

pay Him for anything He's done, but we can show Him how much we appreciate Him and what He does for us — and we can do it every Sunday.

GOD-CENTERED WORSHIP

Think of your church's Sunday morning worship service as one big gathering designed simply to give glory to God for who He is and what He does, and you may find your attitude toward church taking a 180-degree turn.

Hymns will no longer be a bunch of odd words set to organ music, but will become songs to sing with heartfelt enthusiasm because they tell of God's character.

The offering will no longer be a ritual of dropping your loose change into a wooden plate, but will become an expression of your willingness to give back a portion of the money God has given you for His work.

The sermon will no longer be a test of your ability to stay awake, but will become a time to learn more about the gracious God we worship.

And the congregation will no longer be "just a group of people you go to church with," but will become a "family" of believers who are all seeking to glorify God, just like you.

When we can break out of our self-centered way of thinking about church and focus our Sunday morning energy into glorifying God, we take a big step in discovering true worship.

Going to church may not always be the most exciting and entertaining event of your weekend, but it can be the most rewarding.

STAR SEARCH

SEARCH
CHAPTER NINE

The year is 1996, and things in the United States have changed drastically. The newly-elected President turns out to be a fanatical Satan worshiper. But he has a lot of charisma and he's a good politician, so most people don't seem to mind his religion. Using his influence over Congress, he passes a bill designating May 25 as National Satan Day.

On this perverse new holiday, all citizens of the United States are *required* by law to gather together in their local high school gymnasium and, at a predetermined time, bow down to a carved statue of Satan.

For the most part, people don't seem to mind the new holiday. After all, it *is* a day off of work and school. Besides, there is another incentive to participate. . . .

The President, in an amazing display of political clout, has somehow managed to invoke an *immediate* death penalty for anyone who refuses to participate in the holiday ritual. Any person who does not bow down to a Satan statue will face the electric chair within 12 hours. Hundreds of police officers, armed with census information, will be present at each assembly site, noting who is and isn't there.

So, you face a dilemma. You're a Christian, and you know that God expressly forbids you to bow down to any graven image. But if you don't bow down to the statue, you'll be dead before sunrise. What do you do?

THREE MEN AND A FURNACE

As hard to believe as it may sound, this exact (almost) situation happened several thousand years ago. The place was Babylon. Nebuchadnezzar was the king, and he had a bit of a self-image problem. The problem was that he thought of himself as a god.

Not only that, he wanted his subjects to think of him as a god. So he had a 90-foot image of himself made. And he decided that, on a certain day, at a certain time, everyone in the kingdom would assemble in the public square and bow down to worship the image of the king.

As an incentive for his subjects he had a giant furnace erected next to the image and declared that whoever did not bow down to the image would be tossed into the furnace to die a horrible, fiery death.

Shadrach, Meshach, and Abednego were three godly Jews who were living in Babylon at the time of Nebuchadnezzar's decree. And they had a choice to make. To bow down to the image would mean disobeying God; but *not* bowing to the image would mean becoming human kindling.

What could they do?

UNEXPECTED RESULTS

Shadrach, Meshach, and Abednego were young men. They had their whole lives ahead of them. But their loyalty to God outweighed their fear of an early death. When the time came to bow down to the image, these three young Jews remained standing.

When they were seized and brought before the king, they explained that they could worship no one but the *true* God. This enraged the king. True to his word, Nebuchadnezzar immediately had the three young men tossed into the furnace.

But an amazing thing happened — nothing.

Shadrach, Meshach, and Abednego didn't burn. They didn't even break a sweat. As a matter of fact, they strolled around casually in the middle of the flames without becoming the slightest bit uncomfortable!

Of course King Nebuchadnezzar was shocked. When he approached the furnace for a closer look, he saw *four* men in the fire, not three. And one of the men looked like "a son of the gods." Immediately the king had a change of heart. He called for the young men to come out of the furnace. Then, turning to the crowd he said:

Praise be to the God of Shadrach, Meshach, and Abednego, who has sent His angel and rescued His servants! They trusted in Him and defied the king's command and were willing to give up their lives rather than serve or worship any god except their own God. Therefore I decree that the people of any nation or language who say anything against the God of Shadrach, Meshach, and Abednego be cut into pieces and their houses be turned into piles of rubble, for no other god can save in this way.

(Daniel 3:28-29)

As a result of Shadrach, Meshach, and Abednego's decision to follow God's will, King Nebuchadnezzar not only recognized who the *true* God is, he declared Him to be the "official" God of Babylon! In other words, a whole nation was changed by the action of three young men.

HISTORICAL PRECEDENT

Do you think God could ever use you like he used Shadrach, Meshach, and Abednego? Or, let me put it another way: Would you be *willing* to let God use you like He used Shadrach, Meshach, and Abednego?

Don't think that Shadrach, Meshach, and Abednego were superheroes or anything. They were every bit as human as you and I. And it's not like they were elderly men completing a lifetime of godly service. They were *young* men.

But they had one overwhelming personal characteristic. *They were completely dedicated to doing God's will.* And God used their dedication to accomplish great things.

THAT WAS THEN, THIS IS NOW

Would you say you're completely dedicated to doing God's will? If so, get ready for some great things in your life. If not, you might consider it.

God can do great things with your life *right now*. Not when you get older. Now.

A good way to dedicate yourself to His will is to act on the spiritual gifts we discussed in chapter 6. God may never call you to anything as dramatic as facing a fiery furnace; but the *results* of your spiritual gifts could be just as dramatic.

Who knows how many lives you can touch or how many situations you can affect simply by putting to use your God-given abilities. You yourself may never know the far-reaching effect your life has had until you get to heaven.

But God will know. And that's all that matters.

So, let me challenge you to make an impact on your world by allowing God to work through you and by dedicating your life to His will.

GET OUT FROM UNDER THAT BUSHEL

CHAPTER TEN

You're on a camping trip in the Rocky Mountains with a group of your friends. You wake up early one morning and decide to do a little hiking on your own while everyone else is still asleep.

At first, the trail up the mountain is tough. The terrain is rocky (obviously) and you find yourself climbing up grades as steep as 45 degrees. About a mile and a half into the hike, however, the trail begins to level off. Then about a half mile later — to your pleasant surprise — you discover that the trail descends. What a relief to your aching legs!

The gravity of the downhill grade causes you to pick up your pace. As the descent gets steeper, you start to jog. The crisp morning air feels great rushing past your face. You break into a full run. Ahead you see the trail curve off behind a large boulder. You're running full tilt now.

What a life! you think to yourself. Overwhelmed by the rugged beauty all around you, you wish that you could just keep running on this mountain path forever. You approach the curve at full speed.

"STOP!"

The voice seems to come from nowhere. Completely startled, you skid to a halt. Looking around, you see an old man standing on a plateau about ten feet above the path.

"Take a look," he says, nodding toward the curve. "But—be careful!"

You step toward the curve cautiously. Peering around the boulder, you notice something that makes your hands start to shake. Your eyes go wide and your knees start to wobble.

Ahead, not two yards beyond the curve, the trail ends suddenly—*in a 500-foot drop!*

"A rock slide knocked it out about three weeks ago," the old man calls down to you. "I don't know why they haven't closed this trail yet."

Noticing the shaking that has involuntarily taken over your body, he asks, "Are you all right?"

You can't seem to find your voice, so you nod your head.

"Are you by yourself or are you here with someone?" he asks.

"I'm here with some of my friends," you manage to say between deep breaths.

"Well, be sure to tell them about this trail," he calls over his shoulder as he walks away.

So—now you're faced with a choice.

Do you tell your friends about the dangerous trail or do you let them find out about it on their own?

THE TRAIL AND THE CHRISTIAN LIFE

If you're a Christian, you face a similar situation. Think of it this way: If a person has not accepted Jesus as his or her Saviour, he or she is running on a downward path. At the end of that path—unknown to the person—is a drop-off. That drop-off is eternity in hell.

You know about the drop-off. As a matter of fact, you were on the path once yourself—until some caring person told you about the consequences of the path and helped you change directions.

Now that *you* know about the path, are you willing to help others avoid it? Are you willing to share with the unsaved what Jesus has done for you and what He can do for them? I really hope you are. It's a matter of eternal life or death.

Let's take a brief look at how you can be a witness of Christ to people who don't know Him. Basically, there are three levels of Christian witness—the witness of your life, the witness of answers, and active witness.

THE WITNESS
OF YOUR LIFE

"Let your light shine before men, that they may see your good deeds and praise your Father in heaven" (Matthew 5:16).

The way you live your life can be a tremendous witness to people. As a Christian, you've chosen to live your life according to God's plan. This involves participating in activities that are pleasing to Him and avoiding activities that would be displeasing to Him. It involves maintaining a loving attitude toward those who treat you badly. It involves having an inner peace in knowing that, no matter what happens, you have a Heavenly Father looking out for you.

If you live your Christian life displaying such characteristics, other people will notice. They'll begin to recognize you as being different. And they'll begin to wonder what makes you different—what source you get your inner confidence and peace from.

THE WITNESS OF ANSWERS

"Always be prepared to give an answer to everyone who asks you to give the reason for the hope that you have" (1 Peter 3:15).

Not only will people *wonder* what makes you different, they'll *ask* you about it. And your answer could be a great witness.

If someone asked *you* about your Christian life, would you know how to answer? Do you know enough about *why* you believe what you do to explain it to others who ask about it?

If you don't, the obvious place to learn is in the Bible. Think about some of the questions your unsaved friends and family members might ask you about your faith. Then search Scripture for the answers. Anticipating potential questions can help you be prepared to answer them. (For hints on where to look in the Bible for certain topics, check with your parents, youth leader, or some other mature Christian. They'll probably be glad to help you.)

One final point here: Don't worry about having *all* the answers. No one can be expected to immediately answer *every* question he or she is asked. There is nothing wrong with telling someone, "I'm not sure I know the answer to that question right now. Let me check on it and get back to you." Just be sure you follow through on it as soon as possible.

ACTIVE WITNESS

"Go and make disciples of all nations, baptizing them in the name of the Father, and of the Son and of the Holy Spirit" (Matthew 28:19).

When you become comfortable in your ability to answer questions regarding your faith, you're ready to progress to the next level—active witnessing.

Active witnessing is taking the initiative in sharing your faith instead of waiting for someone to ask you about it. To many Christians, this level of witnessing is very intimidating. But it shouldn't be.

As Christians, we have a lot to *share* with our unsaved friends, neighbors, and family members. And that's what we're doing in active witnessing — sharing. We're not trying to cram our beliefs down people's throats. We're simply telling others about the hope, joy, and security we've discovered.

There are many specific methods of sharing your faith and many books and resources available that explain these methods. Ask your youth pastor to help you find these resources.

My goal in writing this chapter has been to point out the urgent need for Christians of all ages to share their faith with those who haven't received Christ as their Saviour.

Remember, we know where the downhill path ends; they don't.

COLD WATER IN A WORLD THAT'S HEATING UP

CHAPTER ELEVEN

If you had been around during the time of Jesus' betrayal, trial, and Crucifixion, would you have done anything to try to help Him?

Think about it. If you had been present in the Garden of Gethsemane, would you have stayed awake and been there to comfort Jesus while the rest of the disciples slept? If you had been present at His trial, would you have helped bandage His wounds after the soldiers had beaten Him? If you had seen Him struggling desperately to carry the cross through the streets of Jerusalem, would you have stepped out of the crowd and helped Him? If you had heard Him say, "I thirst," as He hung on the cross, would you have fetched water for Him to drink?

All of us probably would like to think that we would have offered our assistance to the Saviour as He faced the agony of His Crucifixion. We wouldn't have run away. We wouldn't have deserted Him. We would have stepped forward to comfort Him. We would have done all we could to ease His pain. If we'd only had the opportunity.

Guess what? We *do* have the opportunity.

> Then the King will say . . . "I was hungry and you gave Me something to eat, I was thirsty and you gave Me something to drink, I was a stranger and you invited Me in, I needed clothes and you clothed Me, I was sick and you looked after Me, I was in prison and you came to visit Me."
>
> Then the righteous will answer Him, "Lord, when did we see You hungry and feed You, or thirsty and give You something to drink? When did we see You a

stranger and invite You in, or needing clothes and clothe You? When did we see You sick or in prison and go visit You?"

Then the King will reply, "I tell you the truth, whatever you did for one of the least of these brothers of Mine, you did for Me" (Matthew 25:34-40).

SEEING CHRIST IN OUR WORLD

If you are aware *at all* of the world around you, you know how many hurting people there are. Every day in the news we hear about the plight of the homeless, of the starving masses in Third World countries, of AIDS patients, etc. Today there are more hurting people in need of care than at any other time in history. And if we make an effort to help these hurting people, we are helping Jesus.

We don't have to know all the theological aspects of Jesus' words in Matthew 25:40. If we help the needy, we are helping Jesus. It's as simple as that.

What an incredible opportunity that gives us!

HEARERS AND DOERS

It's easy *not* to get involved with needy and hurting people. When we hear about their plights, it's easy to sit back and say, "Oh, that's too bad—I feel sorry for them" or to say, "I'm glad that's not me." It's easy to be *aware* of their plights, but not personally affected. But that's not the response Christians are called to. Remember, we're not just "hearers," we're "doers."

But my spiritual gift isn't mercy. Am I still responsible to help hurting people?

Good question, and yes, you are.

It would be simple to pass the buck and say only those with certain spiritual gifts are reponsible to help the needy. But it's not true. We're *all* responsible.

Of course, for some, helping hurting people comes more naturally than it

does for others. But we all have contri-
butions we can make to the needy.

WHERE TO START?
With the millions of hurting people in
the world, it's tough to know where to
begin helping. After all, the possibili-
ties are almost endless.

That's why it's important to narrow our
focus. We can't be all things to all
needy people — and we shouldn't try to
be. Instead, we should focus our attention on one or two particular causes.
What areas of concern or particular
groups of hurting people do you feel
most strongly about? Unwed mothers?
The homeless? AIDS patients?

Whatever your answer is, that's where
you should invest your time and effort.

IDEAS TO CONSIDER —
OR NOT
How you choose to respond to hurting
people is up to you. No one knows the

specific circumstances of your community and your life as well as you do. So no one can tell you that "this is exactly what you need to do." But let me offer a few ideas. You may want to try them. You may get some ideas of your own from them. Or you may want to ignore them completely and create your own ideas. It's up to you.

- Start a letter-writing ministry to AIDS patients. Contact your local AIDS awareness organization and explain that you want to begin regular, encouraging correspondence with hospitalized AIDS patients. The organization will probably be glad to put you in touch with the appropriate people. Then begin regularly (perhaps monthly) writing notes of encouragement to these people. (You may also have an opportunity to share your faith in your notes.)

- Set aside a portion of your weekly allowance or paycheck to "sponsor" a child in a Third World country. Many organizations offer such programs.

- Start a fund-raising drive to help a

local shelter for the homeless in your community. To raise the funds, have a car wash, a bake sale, or some other money-making venture.

- Begin a clothing drive among your friends or in your community and distribute the clothes to needy families in your area.

Again, *how* you respond to hurting people is up to you. But it's important that you *do* respond.

There's a world of needy people out there, waiting to be shown Christian love and concern. Let's show them.

Let's not pass up this opportunity to help Christ.

READY TO REIGN

CHAPTER TWELVE

In the first chapter of this book, I listed six "myths" about Christianity:

(1) God is interested in our personal lives;
(2) Jesus is the Son of God;
(3) Jesus rose from the dead;
(4) The Bible is God's Word;
(5) Satan exists;
(6) Non-Christians go to hell.

Of course you probably knew from the start that every one of those statements is true—right? I didn't list them as "myths" to be blasphemous; I did it for another reason. I wanted to startle you into recognizing a fact. The fact is this: There are people and influences in this world that can destroy your faith if you're not prepared for them. With one rational-sounding comment or condescending chuckle, a person may cause you to doubt something you've believed your whole life.

That's why it's important to *personalize* your faith. If your faith is an integral part of you—if you know *what* you believe and *why* you believe it as well as you know your name—no one will be able to shake that faith. (We discussed ways to achieve this kind of faith—Bible study, regular personal devotions, meaningful prayer, etc.—earlier in this book.)

A personalized faith will not only be apparent in your attitude, it will be apparent in your actions. Such actions include using your spiritual gifts, regular worship, witnessing, and helping the needy (all of which, too, have been discussed earlier). A personalized faith will cause you to *live* what you believe.

Exercising your personalized faith not only benefits you, it can also benefit others. And those are very good reasons to exercise your faith. But there's another one.

A SERIOUS EGO BUILDER

I'm not sure whether I should tell you this or not. After all, I wouldn't want to give you a big head. Oh, OK — I'll tell you. . . .

The way *you* exercise *your* faith affects the *entire* Kingdom of God. In fact, as a Christian, *everything you do* either helps or hurts God's Kingdom. Everything. From the friends you choose to the way you spend your free time to the language you use. It all has a bearing on God's Kingdom. That makes you — and the things you do — pretty important. How does that make you feel?

Does it sound like a lot of pressure — to know that the entire Kingdom of God is affected by what you do? Don't worry, no one expects you to be perfect. Unfortunately, we all blow it sometimes and hurt God's Kingdom.

But God is patient and forgiving, and always gives us second chances if we confess our failures to Him. So if we're honestly trying to benefit God's Kingdom, we're in a no-lose situation.

ONE FINAL WORD OF ENCOURAGEMENT

My main goal in writing this book has been to show you that *your* Christian life is important. It's important to you. It's important to your fellow Christians. It's important to the needy people of the world. It's important to the entire Kingdom of God.

It doesn't matter how old you are—you're important. And don't let anyone tell you otherwise.

But with importance comes responsibility. Using the principles we've discussed in this book as a starting point, you can use your importance to accomplish some great things for God's Kingdom.

God has an incredible future planned for you, filled with exciting opportunities. Are you ready for it?